Rainy Day
things to do
with your kids

Faun Harkin

summersdale

Text by Faun Harkin
Illustrations by Alex Hallatt

Summersdale Publishers Ltd
46 West Street
Chichester
West Sussex
PO19 1RP
UK

www.summersdale.com

Printed and bound in Great Britain

ISBN 1 84024 066 0

For Miles

CONTENTS

INTRODUCTION

It's an age-old complaint, but children really do grow up so quickly. One minute you are sitting with your newborn baby in your arms and then *blink* – they're off to school. Blink again and they are taking driving lessons, and before you know it they won't even be back at weekends to get their laundry done.

So instead of relying on the TV to entertain them during their precious early years, why not make the time to have fun with your children while they're still willing. Playing games, teaching young minds new skills and creating priceless memories are the perks of being a parent. I can still remember the activities my mother did with me when I was a child, and can appreciate now how they enriched my childhood. Wouldn't you like your child to be able to say that about you?

The ideas in this book are very simple, require no artistic talent (if they did I wouldn't be able to do them) and use nothing that any parent wouldn't normally have somewhere in their home.

So what are you waiting for – get home and hope for rain!

CLASSICS FOR A NEW GENERATION

How many of us have spent a small fortune on something shiny and plastic for our children that requires 27 batteries, only to find them later playing with the box it came in, the fabulous new toy laying discarded on the floor? All the activities in this section are simple and timeless, and there are plenty of ideas for variations and twists on a classic theme.

When undertaking any activity that requires glue, PVA glue is a must. It is a wonderfully efficient and versatile fixative, and for the untidily creative it dries clear.

A Simple Box

A cardboard box combined with an imagination as vivid as a child's can lead to exciting and limitless possibilities. The following are just a few easy-to-create ideas to provide hours of versatile fun.

What you'll need

- A cardboard box (such as one a new appliance might come in)
- Scissors

Optional:
- Sticky tape
- Pens or paint
- String
- PVA glue
- Blu Tack or similar
- Wrapping paper or wallpaper
- Glitter

What to do

Creating a home

Using a pair of child-friendly scissors, your child can cut windows in the box to turn it into a castle, a fort or a house. Give them some colouring pens or paint and let them go wild adding bricks and bright patterns to their makeshift home.

Creating armour

Cut off the bottom and top of the box so that it will go over your child's head and around their body. Glue or tape two lengths of string from the front to the back, making shoulder straps so that they can move around freely without having to hold up their new armour. They may want to decorate their attire with glitter or paint.

Other ideas

The possibilities for a cardboard box are endless. Your child could turn theirs into a car, an ambulance or an animal – anything they like. A vehicle simply needs wheels, a steering wheel and a 'special powers' button (allowing them to go super fast, fly or be ejected). An animal only requires a painted face and stringy tail, plus the necessary spots or stripes.

TOP TIP

If you have several boxes, why not create a town with your child? Build some houses and shops and cut oblongs of cardboard to make roads. A matchbox glued at one end to a lolly stick and carefully coloured in (glue some paper to the front of the box if necessary) makes a great traffic light, which can be made freestanding by pushing the bottom part into a ball of playdough.

Miles's Board Game

This is probably my favourite rainy day game, and it came about after a badly organised move meant that my son's toys and games were a thousand miles away for four weeks. We decided to try and make our own version of the classic board game.

What you'll need

- Sheet of A3 paper or card
- Pens or crayons
- A ruler
- A dice

What to do

Draw a grid on the paper, dividing it into 64 squares (8 by 8) and numbering each square, starting at the bottom left of the grid. Write forfeits and rewards that are relevant to your child in some of the squares – the sillier the better.

For example:
'Left Teddy on the train – go back to square 15 to get him.'
'Tidied your bedroom – move on 3 places.'
'Put your pants on back to front – miss a go.'
'Shared your toys – move on 5 places.'

Your child can be in charge of colouring in all the squares and adding details such as the snakes, ladders, train and pants.

TOP TIP

If you want to make the game a little harder, include a quiz square: whoever lands on it has to answer a question posed by an opponent. Questions could be on any subject, from TV trivia to maths problems, and you could also include challenges – e.g. Name 5 things which can be found in a bathroom.

QUICK IDEA

Scrapbook Diary

A perfect time-filler for children of almost any age. Keep hold of tickets or leaflets from a day out, and on a rainy day encourage your child to draw a picture of what they did or saw on their trip. Older children can write about the experience, adding details about who came with them, any funny moments and so on. You can add photos and other relevant items, such as leaves or flowers from a country park or a wrist band from a funpark. The scrapbook can be added to regularly.

Make a Time Capsule

The point of a time capsule is to capture a moment in time, so its contents should be personal to your child and relevant to the period in which the capsule is made. I will suggest a few below, but use your imagination – and your child's!

What you'll need

- A biscuit/large chocolate tin (e.g. Roses or Quality Street)
- Pens or crayons
- Paper

What to do

Gather together items that will make great mementoes in a few years' time: for example, a recent photograph of your child; a newspaper dated the day of the activity; pictures or photographs of your child's toys, friends and favourite pop groups; a price list or receipt including everyday items (bread, sweets, toys); a piece of artwork or writing produced by your child... the list is endless. Put all these in the tin and keep your child's time capsule somewhere safe. You could bury it in the garden (remembering where you buried it and to take it with you if you move!), put it in the loft or, as I do, keep it in a memory trunk alongside drawings, babygrows

and school reports. How long you leave it before
opening it up again is entirely up to you.

TOP TIP

Create and complete a questionnaire to go in your
child's time capsule. Sample questions:
What is your favourite food/colour/hobby?
What or who is your favourite toy/band/film star?
Who are your friends?
Why do you like them?
What do you like doing at playtime/after school?
What do you want to be when you grow up?
What is the best thing about being you?
What do you think it will be like in five/ten years' time?
Depending on what electronic wizardry you have
at your disposal, you could film, voice-record
or simply write down your child's answers (or if
old enough get them to fill in the questionnaire
themselves).

Racing Fish

A great game for young siblings – try it at bathtime!

What you'll need

- Thin paper
- Scissors
- Washing up liquid

What to do

Get your children to draw and cut out a fish shape each, about the size of a goldfish. Put it in a washing up bowl half-filled with water or a shallow bath and help them to put tiny drops of washing up liquid behind the fish (in the V of its tail). Make sure the liquid does not touch the paper fish. The fish will move forwards away from the washing up liquid and the first fish to reach the other side of the bowl or bath wins!

TOP TIP

You can make this more interesting for older children by putting floating items into the water to create walls and dead ends, like a maze. Watch your children have fun trying to navigate their fish through it!

OUT AND ABOUT

Large or National Museums

Children have always groaned at the idea of visiting a museum, but go to one today and children can experience history, technology and science in a fully hands-on way. They can perform scientific experiments and literally touch the past for themselves. The key to a successful museum trip is advance preparation. Pick the museum that you think will most interest your child – perhaps following on from a topic at school or something they've seen on television. Put your child in charge by giving them a map of the museum and asking them where they would like to go and what they would like to see. Add to this your own preferences and give your child the role of guiding you through the museum, deciding on a route that best ensures everyone gets to see what they want to see. Set a time limit for each area and give your child a watch – being timekeeper will afford them little opportunity to get bored!

Puppet Theatre

As a child I played with a collection of puppets that my mother owned. The set didn't always have the exact character I needed for a story, which meant that a dragon often stood in for the wicked wolf in *Little Red Riding Hood*!

What you'll need

- Puppets (hand puppets are best – there is a section on making them in this book)
- A large box (one that a washing machine or TV comes in is ideal – ask an electrical store for a spare if you don't have one)
- A3 paper
- PVA glue
- Plain-coloured wallpaper or wrapping paper
- Pens or paint
- Scissors
- Sticky tape
- Blu Tack
- Ruler

What to do

Sit the box on one of its shorter sides so that it is at its tallest. Cut the flaps off at the back so your child (or children) can sit or kneel inside the box. Decorate the outside of the box with wallpaper, wrapping paper or paint. You can use a ruler and pen to measure out the paper for greater accuracy, but this isn't essential. Cut out the top half of the front of the box – this will be the window or 'stage' through which the hand puppets will appear.

Before discarding the cut-out cardboard, use it as a template to cut out an identically sized piece of paper. Ask your child (or children) to pick a story, or even make up their own, and draw a scene on the paper to create a backdrop – a forest, a kitchen, a castle, a garden: whatever the story requires (perhaps more than one). Hang the scene inside the box with sticky tape so that it is visible to the 'audience', but leave enough of a gap for your child's hand to fit between the paper and the front of the box.

Now all that's needed is to practise telling the story through the puppets and narration. Finally, find some willing family members or friends to be the audience and let the show begin!

Marble Maze

Remember those frustrating pocket games where you had to gently guide a ball bearing through a maze to a finish point? You can create a larger version with your child!

What you'll need

- A shoebox
- Card
- PVA glue
- Sticky tape
- A marble

What to do

Cut the card into a range of rectangular lengths, about 4 cm tall and no longer than half the length of the box. These will be the walls of your maze. Cut 1-cm-deep slits at regular intervals along each strip. Fold out these 'tabs' in alternate directions so they can be glued to the bottom of the box to create a stable wall. It's easier if you start with a long piece first to make a corridor, and then add the other pieces to make your maze. Your objective is to devise a route for the marble from a start point to a finish point, so arrange pieces with that in mind: put some walls together to create corners, and in other cases leave a gap, like a gate, for the marble to roll through. Create dead ends so that the marble will simply roll to the edge of the box and have to come back again.

Make sure that only one route will take you from the start point to the finish point, and label these points clearly by gluing a card sign to the relevant part of the shoebox. All that remains is for the player to place the marble at the Start and carefully tilt the box to lead it to the Finish.

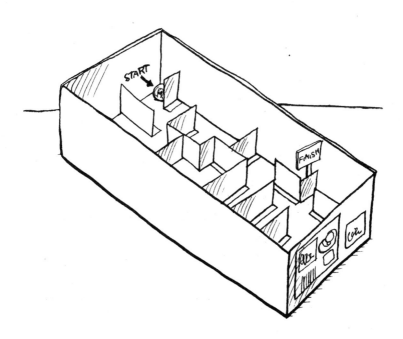

HOME RECORDING STUDIO

Children love to hear themselves on tape and all of these activities will keep them amused for hours. For each one you will need a tape recorder and a blank, recordable cassette, as well as the additional items listed. Alternatively you could use a PC microphone or camcorder, if you have these.

Read-along Books

This is a variation on an idea my mother came up with, having reread my favourite books for the hundredth time. I suggest using a story book, but why don't you and your child also try making up a story yourselves? That way you can include as many 'sound effect' possibilities as you like.

What you'll need

- A story book
- Various household items

What to do

Have your child practise reading the story before hitting the record button. If your child is too young to read the story, read it yourself and encourage them to contribute by adding sound effects, making use of things you'll find in the house:

- Closing and opening doors
- Stamping to make footsteps
- Rustling paper to make crunching leaf sounds
- Clanging pots and pans together to make thunder, trips and crashes

- Scraping a pen over a comb to make a zipping sound
- Dropping marbles or pebbles into a tin to make rain or rockfalls

Once you have recorded your child's ear-pleasing story, rewind the tape and listen, as often as you like.

TOP TIP

You could record several stories and create a mini library for your child – particularly helpful on long car journeys.

The activity also works well as a calming down game at a party, since quiet is needed to hear the sound effects.

Household Band

This is a good activity to get siblings playing nicely as the more committed they are to working as a team the more fun the band will be. It doesn't matter if the results are far from harmonic – children love hearing music they themselves have created.

What you'll need (and how to play)

Guitar
- Lidless shoebox or tissue box
- Elastic bands
- Empty kitchen roll tube
- Sticky tape

Stretch the bands over the box and strum or pluck them. Vary the size of the bands to achieve different pitches. For the finishing touch, secure the kitchen roll tube to one of the shorter ends of the box with sticky tape to represent the fret board.

Drums
- Saucepans, tins (e.g. biscuit), plastic or metal bowls
- Wooden spoons
- Pastry brush

Simply lay the saucepans, tins or bowls upside down around the child so they can bang them with the wooden spoons. They can also create great skiffle band sounds by sliding the pastry brush over the base of the upturned objects.

Maracas
- Empty jam jar with lid
- Uncooked pasta or rice

Half fill the jar with pasta or rice and then screw the lid on tightly. Gently shaking the jar will create that familiar 'rainfall' sound.

Zither/washboard
- Hair comb
- Pencil

Scrape the pencil point up and down the teeth of the comb.

Xylophone (for older/more sensible children!)
- 4 or 5 glass bottles (e.g. milk bottles)
- Wooden spoon

Fill each bottle with a different amount of water – when the child taps the side of each one gently with a wooden spoon, you should hear a distinct note.

This 'instrument' requires a good deal of skill and care to avoid spillages or accidents, so if you are at all uncertain about your child's ability to play it safely, do not include it.

What to do

The band members need to choose a song, listen to it a few times if you have a recorded copy, and practise their own dulcet version. Hit the record button and before the band begins, introduce each musician and their instrument (for example, 'Over here on drums we have little Billy Bloggs…').

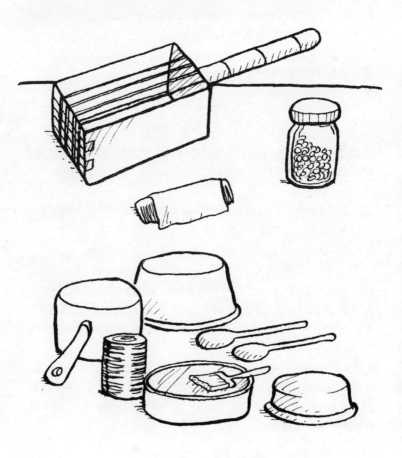

QUICK IDEA

Musical Hats

Musical chairs can get boisterous and out of hand, especially if there is a large group of children. For a gentler version, you just need a hat – one belonging to an adult is best as it will be easy to put on and take off quickly.

Simply sit the children in a circle and give one the hat. While the music is playing they must put the hat on properly and then pass it to the next person – this continues until the music stops. Whoever is wearing or holding the hat at that point leaves the circle. Continue until you have a winner.

Name That Song

This is another game of my mother's, this time to encourage better listening skills in me as a child. My son prefers to 'Name That Book' and is able to spot stories from just a sentence or two.

What you'll need

- A (children's) music tape or CD
- Several children's story books
- Bells, whistles or other noise-making toys

What to do

The simple, original version of the activity is to play the introductory few seconds to a song and ask your child to guess what they are listening to. If they can't guess correctly straight away, play another few seconds until they identify the song, then move on to the next one.

For another round of the game, play pre-recorded sounds such as a tap running, a toilet flushing, or any of the sound effects or instruments mentioned elsewhere in this section.

Another variation is to read the first sentence of a story your child is familiar with (and the second, third and so on) until they give you the correct title. You will need to keep the books concealed (e.g. behind a larger one) for this round!

TOP TIP

If more than one child is playing, give each one a bell, whistle or similar and tell them to sound their 'buzzer' when they think they recognise the sound. Award points simply by giving one per correct answer, or make it more interesting by handing them out on a sliding scale, depending on how much of the sound was heard before the correct answer was given. At the end of the game the person with the most points wins.

Dance and Interpretation

This was another favourite of mine as a child, and encourages imagination as well as an early appreciation of classical music.

What you'll need

- A classical or instrumental music tape or CD – or even a radio programmed to a relevant music station

What to do

Play the music to your child and let them imagine what it is portraying. Encourage them to move and dance with the music, perhaps turning himself or herself into the creature it reminds them of, or move in the way the music flows. With younger children you need to get up and join in, for the first tune at least, giving them a few ideas on the animal or mood the music might represent.

The music you choose should be as obvious as possible – 'Night on the Bare Mountain' is a great one for encouraging some witch and broomstick fun, while 'The Blue Danube Waltz' could lead to living room scenes involving swans or boats.

ARTS AND CRAFTS

Getting your hands messy with your child is a wonderful way to spend a rainy day – not only does it develop your son's or daughter's creative and expressive skills, but the resulting artefacts will also be a permanent window back into their childhood.

As mentioned before, PVA glue should be an essential item in every parent's crafts kit.

Shell Pots

This idea came about from spending wet holidays in Britain as a child. On the occasional sunny days we went to the beach and collected shells, and then we spent the wet days decorating pots and frames. My mother still has the shell pot I made in 1978.

What you'll need

- Some shells
- Putty (try aquatic shops for the green fish tank putty as this is usually safer than the window variety)
- A plant pot (terracotta or plastic)
- A skewer
- Non-toxic varnish or PVA glue
- A small paintbrush

What to do

The number of shells needed will depend on the size of the plant pot. Cover the outside of the pot in putty and get your child to decorate it with the shells they have collected, pushing them firmly into the putty. When they are happy with their work, they can use a skewer to dot in their name and the date wherever there is a gap in the shells.

Leave the pot somewhere warm and dry until the putty has hardened and then you, not the child, should varnish it (using the paintbrush) to keep the shells in place. If you don't have varnish, use watered down PVA glue instead – this makes a splendid shiny coating.

OUT AND ABOUT

Small or Local Museums

Local museums can be magical places, particularly ones where the curators have not grouped items together in the orderly fashion of a larger museum, meaning you can never be sure what is around the next corner. Full of photographs of landmarks and streets taken many generations ago, local museums will fascinate young children and help them understand how their community has changed. Ask your child if they can recognise any of the streets in the photos – you can help by pointing out familiar buildings or a particular road layout. Discuss with your child how buildings have been altered, trees have grown and shops have changed. If there are people in the photograph you could ask your child to guess roughly when it was taken, concealing any details that might give the answer away.

Some museums produce information sheets for schools, which you can easily adapt for your child's age if necessary.

Picture Frame

With a little bit of help, children can make creatively personalised frames for their favourite photographs or drawings.

What you'll need

- 2 pieces of cardboard (A5 size)
- A pencil
- A ruler
- Decorations (glitter, shells, leaves, sequins, ribbons, bows, thread, fabric – anything!)
- PVA glue
- A paintbrush
- Scissors

What to do

Take one of the A5 pieces of card and, with a ruler, mark a line an inch from each edge, creating a smaller rectangle inside. Cut the smaller rectangle out and discard it (or keep for the Top Tip). You have now made the top part of the frame. Brush PVA glue over the frame and let your child decorate it. Fill in the gaps with glitter (or sand, if your child would like to make a seaside-themed frame to mount a holiday drawing they have done).

When it is dry, paint on a layer of PVA glue mixed with a little water to help keep the glitter and decorations in place.

When the glue is dry the frame is ready to be put together. Attach the decorated part to the second piece of card with a thin strip of glue to the bottom and two sides. You should then be able to slip a photograph or picture down into the gap between the two pieces of card.

TOP TIP

Make a stand for the frame from the leftover card. Ensure it is a couple of inches wide, for stability, and glue it to the back of the frame so that it can be displayed free-standing.

Pebble Painting

This makes a perfect holiday rainy day activity and is also a lovely memento of your trip. If you don't have all the materials while you're away, put the pebbles somewhere safe and save the activity for a rainy day at home.

What you'll need

- Small pebbles (from the beach)
- Poster or acrylic paint/non-toxic permanent markers
- Non-toxic varnish or PVA glue and water mixture
- Paintbrushes

What to do

Clean the pebble and dry it thoroughly. Get your child to decorate one side of it using markers or paint. Arty children can create a picture, e.g. of the chalet or town you stayed in. When it is dry, help your child to put their name and the date and place the pebble came from on the other side. When it is dry, varnish it using the non-toxic varnish or by brushing PVA glue mixed with water onto it.

The pebble is a lovely decoration for any display cabinet, or it can be used as a pretty paperweight. A perfect souvenir gift for grandparents!

Papier Mâché Hat

There is so much you can do with papier mâché – this is one simple item to get you going, but have a go at making other things too and you will find you can be very resourceful. My son and I have made car ramps and even a door-knocker!

What you'll need

For the papier mâché:
- PVA glue and water mixture (7 parts to 3)
- Newspaper torn into strips
- A paintbrush

For the hat:
- A tape measure
- A compass
- PVA glue
- Paper or card (the larger the better – A3 or bigger)
- Sticky tape
- Scissors

Measure the circumference of your child's head, add 4 cm (to allow for shrinkage as the glue dries), and cut a sheet of card or paper to the length. This will be the top part of the hat, so unless you want a really tall hat, you might want to cut it down to fit your child better. Now tape the ends together to make a tube.

Stand the tube on another piece of paper or card and draw a circle around it. Draw a slightly bigger circle around that one with a 1-cm margin between circles (use a compass for accuracy), and then cut out the bigger circle. Cut 1-cm slits around the edge of the circle (up to the pencil mark) to create tabs that you can fold down and glue to the inside of one end of the tube. Now you have the hat's 'lid' in place.

Again draw around the tube onto paper or card and this time draw a slightly smaller circle within that one with a 1-cm margin between circles. Now draw a much larger circle around both of these, exactly how much larger depending on how big your child wants the brim to be. Cut around the largest and smallest circles so you are left with a doughnut-style ring. Attach the brim to the open end of the tube in the same way as before, cutting 1-cm strips about 2 cm apart around the inside of the brim and gluing these to the inside of the tube.

Leave the glue to dry, then get your child to paste strips of newspaper onto the hat using the paintbrush and the PVA/water mixture. No more than two layers are necessary. Allow a couple of hours for this to dry and then let your child paint whatever colours or design they want onto the hat. When that has dried, the hat is ready to wear.

QUICK IDEA

Cut-out Faces

Gather together a number of newspapers and magazines and cut out facial features, such as eyes, ears, noses, lips, eyebrows and hair – the more unusual and funny the better.

When you have a selection, draw a large oval on an A4 sheet of paper and place the cut-outs on it, mixing them up to create wacky faces. You can glue the features on for a permanent Picasso-esque piece of art or simply keep changing them.

With younger children you could ask them to look for 'happy' eyes or 'sad' mouths to help improve their recognition skills. They could even try to make a face that looks like someone they know.

Spy Messages

This is a game I used to play with my son when he was learning to read. An ordinary pencil-length candle can be used very effectively, and is less likely to break when pressed heavily against a sheet of paper by sweaty little hands!

What you'll need

- White paper
- A white wax crayon or plain candle
- Felt tip pens or paint

What to do

Write a message or draw a picture on the paper using the crayon or candle, then ask your child to reveal the secret message by painting or drawing all over the page. You can also encourage your child to guess what the message or drawing is going to be while you are creating it.

Then swap roles so it's now you who has to reveal your child's secret creation.

Funky Fabric

This is easy to do. My son loves trying his hand at some creative designing and the results are always worth the effort. The ironing part is strictly for adults only, but the rest the child can do him- or herself.

What you'll need

- 2 sheets of greaseproof paper
- 2 small pieces, about 10 cm by 10 cm, of bubble wrap (with small bubbles)
- Little bits of paper, confetti, glitter, leaves and other decorations
- An iron

What to do

Put one piece of the bubble wrap on the table and let your child decorate it by sprinkling the paper, confetti etc. over it. Then put the second piece of bubble wrap on top and sandwich the whole thing between the sheets of greaseproof paper. Take the sandwiched fabric carefully to the ironing table and run an iron on its coolest setting over each side to fuse the bubble wrap together. Let it cool and then remove the greaseproof paper to reveal the masterpiece! You can make several of these and add to fancy dress costumes.

Make a Puppet

Puppets are great at firing children's imaginations but can be costly. Why not make some simple, inexpensive and unique puppets? Remember that if you are allowing your child to sew, use blunt darning needles so that they don't prick their fingers.

What you'll need

Finger and hand puppets:
- Fabric (from a fabric shop or old clothes)
- Marker pen or (tailor's) chalk
- Needle and thread
- Wool and sequins to decorate
- Glue
- Scissors

Stringed puppets:
- String
- Floppy or rag dolls
- A5 piece of cardboard cut into the shape of a capital T

What to do

Finger puppet

Cut out from the material two U-shaped pieces approximately double the width and matching the length of your child's middle and index fingers put together. These pieces will make the body of the puppet. Sew a small hem around three edges, leaving the short straight edge open (so that they can put their fingers in) and turn the puppet inside out. Sew or glue on wool for hair and beards, and sequins for facial features. If you are very arty add smaller bits of material for clothes, hats and so on.

Hand puppet

Draw around your child's hand in a mitten shape, adding about 2 cm to the width and height of the hand as you go. Remember that hand puppets have two arms so include these features when drawing the outline (big enough to fit your child's thumb and little finger inside when sewn). Sew up and decorate in the same way as the finger puppets.

Stringed puppet

This is slightly more complicated, and requires a rag doll or unarticulated toy (e.g. one without joints) to complete. Picture a traditional stringed puppet and this will help you.

Tie lengths of string around the wrists and knees and sew lengths to the backside and head of the toy. Tape the string from the knees to the horizontal length of the T-board so that by rocking the board from left to right the legs rise and fall as though walking.

Attach the string from the hands on the same piece of board as the knees, but a little closer to the ends and on slightly longer bits of string – that way they will not lift when you rock the T-board. You will be able to move the hands by tilting the board in a slightly different direction (practice is key!).

Attach the toy's bottom to the foot of the T so that tipping the bar forward will make the puppet bend over.

Adjust the length of the strings as necessary so that the toy will move just how you want it to when you tilt the T-board this way and that.

Make a Book

A book is very simple to make and can be a lovely gift for a friend or relative, or something to be included in a time capsule.

What you'll need

- A4 or A5 paper (several sheets)
- Pens and pencil
- A ruler
- A stapler

What to do

Discuss with your child the kind of story they would like to write – for example, an adventure or fantasy story, or even a memory of a holiday or visit to a zoo.

Positioning each sheet of paper 'portrait', divide in half horizontally with a straight pencil line and draw more lines on the bottom half of the pages for your child to use as a writing guide. The child should then write the story on the bottom half of the pages and illustrate the top half of the pages. Use both sides of the paper and add page numbers.

Next, get your child to design a front and back cover, making sure that they include their name.

Have them look at their favourite story books to see how the covers are laid out and what other information is featured, such as a story synopsis (or 'blurb'), price, something about the author and an International Standard Book Number, or ISBN (you'll find this above a barcode at the bottom of any book's back cover – have your child make one up for their own book).

Put the pages in order and staple the whole thing together along the left, about one-third and two-thirds down.

TOP TIP

If an older child wants to do a longer book, or create a compendium of stories over time, why not take the pages, unstapled, to a print shop, where they will bind it all professionally for roughly the price of a cappuccino.

OUT AND ABOUT

Country Houses

The more you can bring to life the fact that the country house you are visiting was once a family home, the more your child will gain from the trip. Before you go, discuss the daily lives of boys and girls who once lived or worked in the house, pointing out the differences between their lifestyles and considering what the cause of that might have been. Ask them what commodities wouldn't yet have been invented (for example, central heating, television, vacuum cleaners, baths with running water) and ask them how the family coped without these.

By the time you reach the house your child should be bursting to see for themselves how their young counterparts lived and investigate bathrooms or check out portraits on the walls.

Make a Family Newspaper

These make excellent 'round-up' newsletters that are perfect for family and friends at Christmas.

What you'll need

- Paper (A4 and A3 ideally)
- Pens
- Glue
- A newspaper
- Instant coffee and water (optional)

What to do

Main story: Help your children to recreate an amusing but true tale that has happened in your family, such as a lost pet found safely or an amusing DIY disaster. This works best if written in the style of a newspaper article: 'There was dust and bricks everywhere,' said a spokesperson for the injured father of two.

Adverts: Create funny adverts for items that are relevant to your family – such as Aunt Flo's Memory Cure (for a particularly forgetful sibling), or Dr Johnson's Wide-awake Syrup (for an overworked mum). You can also make a quiz or a crossword with clues again relevant to your family.

Sports: You can have a sports section based on daily family activities – for example, an older sibling's record-breaking achievement in the Most Time Spent in the Bathroom competition, or Dad's unlucky defeat at the Taxi Driver of the Year finals, losing to a more punctual contestant.

Cartoons: Your children can create cartoon strips too, by drawing pictures in small square boxes that recount a family event in snapshot form. You can write in any story points or speech bubbles if your child is too young to do so.

When you have completed the pieces help your children cut them out and arrange them on the sheet of A3 paper in the same way that a newspaper is laid out. Glue the pieces down. You can age your paper by putting half a teaspoon of coffee granules or some brown paint in a bowl and adding cold water until the mixture is pale brownish-yellow in colour. Using a cotton wool ball gently wipe a tiny amount of the solution over the paper and leave to dry.

TOP TIP

For added effect create headlines from newspaper print in the style of a tabloid paper. For example:

- MUM IN BURNT CAKE INCIDENT
- BOY OF 6 IN NO-STABILISERS RIDING SENSATION
- FATHER ACCUSED OF SHOCKING 'DAD DANCING' AT FAMILY WEDDING
- GIRL, 8, IN MISSING SCRUNCHIE DRAMA

FAMILY NEWS

FIDO EATS CAKE

EYEWITNESS REPORT

EAT YOUR PEAS SAYS MUM

EDITOR

Make Paper Beads

These easy-to-make beads can be turned into a unique and colourful accessory, which your child can either wear or give as a present for someone else.

What you'll need

- Newspaper/wrapping paper/plain paper
- Scissors
- A thin metal knitting needle (or skewer)
- Playdough
- Glue
- A paintbrush
- Paints (optional)
- Thin string or elastic cord

What to do

Cut the paper into long strips of varying widths, between 1 and 3 cm. For rounded beads taper the paper gradually at both ends – the strip will look like an elongated diamond. For unusual-shaped beads, cut a long V into the strips, as though creating a long forked tongue. Wind each strip around the needle, brushing the glue onto the paper (avoiding the needle) as you wind. Then slip the paper beads off the needle and leave to dry.

Meanwhile, wrap some string or elastic cord loosely around your child's head over the ears, add 4 cm to the length and cut. For a bracelet, wrap some elastic around their wrist, remembering to add 4 cm to the length, and then cut.

If you have used newspaper or plain paper, paint the beads whatever colour or pattern you like. When the paint has dried, thread the beads onto the string or cord until there is only 5 cm left and then tie into a knot. This should now fit over your child's head or hand as a necklace or bracelet.

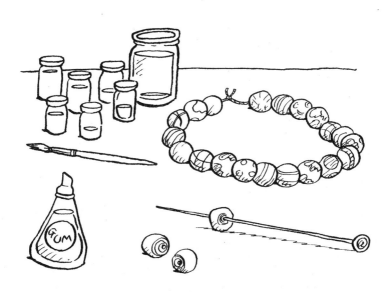

QUICK IDEA

What the Moon Said

All you need for this game is a piece of paper, some pens and two or more people.

Create a 'love story', taking it in turns to write each part and folding over the page so that the next person cannot see what you have written. Include the following parts:

- A girl's name
- A boy's name
- Where they met
- What she said to him
- What he said to her
- What happened next
- Then finally what the moon says. This is usually a moral or comment on the events – for example: 'That's what you get for falling in love'; 'I knew it was meant to be'; or 'All's fair in love and war'.

Two-in-One Pictures

The best pairing of pictures for this activity include one of yourself or your child and one of something funny such as a chimpanzee – watch as you turn into a chimp and back again!

What you'll need

- Two pictures or photos of the same size
- Card
- A ruler
- A pencil
- PVA glue
- Sticky tape

What to do

Mount each picture onto card with glue. Using a ruler and pencil, cut each picture into 10 strips of equal width. Working from left to right, label the strips from the first photo 1 to 10 and those from the second A to J. Arrange the strips in pairs, one from each photo, with odd strips at either end. In front of you now you should have:

A / 1B / 2C / 3D / 4E / 5F / 6G / 7H / 8I / 9J / 10

Turn the paired strips over and tape together along the length, so that although joined they are still flexible and a hinge is created between the two partial images. Next, a good lesson in accuracy and eye–hand coordination; cut 20 equilateral triangles out of card (tip: measure one, cut it out, then use it as a template for the rest). The sides should be equal to the width of a single picture strip. Tape a card triangle at both ends of each of the paired strips (folded), placing one of the triangle points in the join of the strips. Each of the paired strips should now resemble a Toblerone bar in shape.

Cut the remaining two triangles in half and attach to the single strips that are on the left and right of the picture (A and 10). Now take another piece of card big enough to use as a backing for your creation. Glue or tape the strips in order onto the backing card.

When completed you should be able to view one picture from the left and another from the right.

PAINTING

Painting is something we parents think of first when trying to amuse our children. However, not all of us are blessed with a natural skill with a paintbrush. Here are some ideas to make some different paint effects; perfect for small children and artistically-challenged parents!

Bubbles

My son loves making these, not just because he thinks that they look like the craters on the moon, but also because it requires blowing bubbles with a straw – something he's usually forbidden to do!

What you'll need

- Poster paint
- Washing up liquid
- Empty ice cream tub
- Plastic drinking straw
- Paper

What to do

In an empty ice cream tub (or something of a similar shape) mix water with a squirt of paint and a squirt of washing up liquid. The tub should be full almost to the brim with this watery mixture, so it's best to do it over a sink or bath. Get your child to blow into the mixture with a straw until a layer of bubbles appears (be very careful they don't breathe in!). Next they need to lay a piece of paper on top, very gently so as to keep the bubbles as intact as possible. Lift the paper off carefully and marvel at the bubble effect.

Snail Trails

This is a very simple effect to achieve but children love the slimy trails that result.

What you'll need

- Washing up bowl
- Paper plate
- Marble
- Poster paint
- Paper

What to do

Put a piece of paper in an empty washing up bowl. Meanwhile, put a marble on a paper plate with a little paint and cover the marble in the paint (your child will enjoy this task). Then put the marble in the bowl and tip the bowl so that it rolls around all over the paper.

TOP TIP

For a worm trail effect, drag a length of string (instead of a marble) through some paint and then drag the string over a piece of paper.

OUT AND ABOUT

Art Galleries

If you are keen to visit an art gallery, there's no reason why your child should miss out on the experience.

If there is any pointillist art on show, a child will think it great fun if you cover their eyes and bring them as close as you can to the canvas. Then remove your hand so that all they can see are some dots right in front of them. Finally let them walk backwards slowly, until they can see what the image is.

If you are desperate to stay in one area for a while and need to keep your child occupied, get them to count legs. On each painting they must count every pair of legs on the people and animals portrayed and work out which painting in the room has the highest leg count. This can take some time and requires lots of concentration – a perfect aid to parent art appreciation.

Marble Effect

This is easy to do and the marbled paper you end up with is every bit as fancy as the kind found in the shops (which can sell for several pounds for a single sheet!).

What you'll need

- Empty ice cream tub
- Paint
- Oil (e.g. any cooking oil)
- Spoon

What to do

Fill the ice cream tub with water and add a dollop of paint and a splash of oil. Swirl gently with a spoon. Put the paper onto the surface of the water and very carefully lift if off without sliding. A very striking visual effect will be achieved. Using more than one colour will produce an even funkier look!

Hand Painting

The resulting work of art after trying this golden oldie is a great memento of how little your child's hands used to be.

What you'll need

- Poster paint
- Spray bottle
- Paper

What to do

If your child likes to do finger or hand painting, put the paint into a clean and empty spray bottle – one that's used for spraying plants is ideal. You may need to water the paint down a little if it is too thick to be sprayed as it is. Make sure your child is wearing old clothes and then let them spray the paint from a close distance onto their hands, which should be laid flat – face up – on some newspaper. Ensure that they hold the nozzle away from their faces at all times. They can do a simple handprint or create anything they like using their fingers as paintbrushes. Remember to have them write their name and the date on the picture.

OUT AND ABOUT

Time Traveller

This is a game I used to play with my mother when we went on days out and it always added a new dimension to the experience for me. On the way to a country house, tell your child that they are a time traveller who, at the end of the day, will go back in time to visit a child (e.g. Arthur) who once lived in the old house. Explain that when they see Arthur it will be to alert him to some imminent danger, such as a fire, and they must prove they know about Arthur's future in order to save his life. By thinking about what has been invented since the house was built and knowing the history of the family who lived there, your child will be able to show that they have seen Arthur's future and convince him that they are telling the truth.

On the way home, take on the role of a suspicious Arthur while your child tells you everything they have learned at the house.

FUN IN THE KITCHEN

There are some things that you just *have* to do with your children at least once – such as creating erupting volcanos or playing with home-made slime. Instead of breaking the bank to buy expensive ready-made kits, impress your children by turning your kitchen into a science lab, and save your pennies for another rainy day. There's a big kid in all of us and, if you are like me, you will have as much fun as your child with these messy and spectacularly entertaining ideas.

Make Playdough

Commercial playdough is OK, although curiously tempting for very small children to eat. This recipe is foolproof as it contains no chemicals, is made entirely of edible ingredients and tastes foul.

What you'll need

- 6 oz (150 g) plain (all-purpose) flour
- 3 oz (75 g) salt
- 2 tbsp cream of tartar
- 2 tbsp vegetable oil
- ½ pint (250 ml) water with 2–3 drops of any food colouring

What to do

Put the flour, salt, oil and cream of tartar into a bowl and mix well with a wooden spoon. Add the water slowly, as you may not need all of it. When it begins to form a firm dough, knead gently until it is smooth and malleable. Now it is ready for play!

When your child has finished playing, wrap the dough tightly in cling film to keep it soft for next time. Alternatively you can leave it out to harden overnight if your child creates something they want to keep.

Salt Dough Creations

My son and I make the dough together as there are no dangerous ingredients involved, but I find he gets far more pleasure from the creating and baking part.

What you'll need

- 8 oz (200 g) salt
- 8 oz (200 g) flour
- ¼ pint (125 ml) water (room temperature)
- Varnish

What to do

Put the flour and salt into a large mixing bowl and get your child to mix them gently as the water is gradually added. Eventually it will bind together and when a very rough dough forms, help your child to bash, roll and knead it until it becomes smooth. Your dough is ready to get creative with now!

Show your child how to make a simple shape to get them started, such as a snake (break off a small piece and roll it into a long thin sausage). Help them with their creations, perhaps by adding features to faces, which if made very slightly damp, will stick to the rest of the figure before being baked. There are lots of things you can do with salt dough, such as plaiting it into long ribbons, or making dollies or animals.

Place on a baking tray in a preheated oven, at 120 °C for 3–4 hours, depending on how large the creation is. Tap the base to check it is cooked through: a hollow sound is what you are looking for. When it is cool, varnish the creation for a longer-lasting finish, and to protect the dough from mould.

TOP TIP

Make Christmas tree decorations by rolling out the dough and using pastry cutters. After baking, leave to cool and then paint (try sprinkling glitter on while still wet). Leave to dry before varnishing and again leaving to dry. Finally glue a loop of string to the back and hang from a branch of the Christmas tree.

QUICK IDEA

Life-sized Picture

Get your child to lie down on the underside of some wallpaper and draw round them. Then give them some colouring pens and let their imaginations fly! They could put themselves in a uniform, a superhero outfit or anything they like.

When it is finished stick the picture on their bedroom wall – as the months go by they will be fascinated by how much they've grown.

Make Bubble Liquid

It isn't expensive to buy bubble liquid, but once you've tested the hard-core bubble-making power of the home-made variety, you will never go back!

What you'll need

- ¼ pint (125 ml) washing up liquid
- ½ pint (250 ml) water
- 2 tbsp glycerine
- Bottles
- Drinking straws/garden wire/bag ties

What to do

Carefully mix the ingredients together in a measuring jug by swirling gently; you do not want the solution to get too bubbly at this stage! Pour into old bubble bottles or any bottles with necks which aren't too narrow. For best results leave overnight.

Use drinking straws to make little bubbles by dipping one end of the straw into the solution and then blowing it carefully into the air. If you have any garden wire or bag ties, you can easily twist these into effective bubble wands.

TOP TIP

Create large bubbles with a cone of paper dipped into the solution so that a thin layer is spread across the larger opening of the cone. The solution will need to be in a bigger container, such as the measuring jug or a tub. Go outside once it's dark and shine a torch underneath the big bubbles to create a stunning effect.

Make a Volcano

This is a favourite of my son's as it gives an instant and satisfyingly messy result.

What you'll need

- Newspaper
- Plasticine or playdough
- 1 tbsp bicarbonate of soda
- Red food colouring
- Washing up liquid
- 4 tbsp (60 ml) vinegar

What to do

Cover a tabletop with newspaper. Get your child to create the volcano using playdough or plasticine, the structure being big enough to include a concave top about the size of a small coffee cup. Put the bicarbonate of soda into this dip and add 2 or 3 drops of red food colouring. Then add 2 or 3 drops of washing up liquid. Standing back a little, pour in the vinegar (your child will probably want to do this part!). The red lava will erupt and dribble down the sides of the volcano.

Slime

Children should be involved in the playing but not the making! Slime is quick and easy to make but the preparation is strictly for adults only.

What you'll need

- 1 pint (500 ml) water
- 3 oz (75 g) cornflour
- Food colouring (green is an obvious choice!)

What to do

Bring the water to a boil in a medium-sized saucepan. Add the cornflour then the food colouring while stirring constantly. Remove from the heat and cool to room temperature.

This makes a messy slime that goes from liquid to solid, and is great fun to play with.

Always store in an airtight bag in the fridge – slime goes mouldy very quickly when handled with grubby little hands.

BAKING

Give a child a wooden spoon and the result is always messy, but the more they practise the better they become. Taking the time to show your children how to cook is a productive way to spend a wet afternoon and it might even create a passion that lasts a lifetime. At the very least it will be a skill that will prove very useful in later life! Remember to exercise common sense in all baking activities and don't let your child carry out potentially dangerous tasks, such as handling hot items and doing anything at the stove. Anything which is baked should be left to cool on a wire rack as soon as it leaves the oven.

Gingerbread Cut-outs

This is my mother's recipe for perfect gingerbread men which produces wonderfully dark-coloured biscuits that melt in the mouth, rather than the paler, tooth snapping offerings resulting from other recipes.

What you'll need

- 3 oz (75 g) black treacle
- 4 oz (100 g) margarine
- 8 oz (200 g) soft dark sugar
- 2 tbsp milk
- 1 lb (500 g) plain flour
- 1 tbsp ground ginger
- 1 tbsp bicarbonate of soda
- Raisins
- Pastry cutter

What to do

Pre-heat the oven to 180 °C. Ask your child to grease two large baking sheets and then help you to measure all the dry ingredients, and put them into separate bowls in readiness.

Put the treacle, margarine, sugar and milk into a small saucepan and melt over a gentle heat. When the mixture is cool, get your child to sift the flour, ginger and bicarbonate of soda into a bowl. Hold the now cool saucepan over the bowl and ask them to mix as you add the treacle mixture. Help them to stir the mixture until it forms a smooth dough.

Put the dough onto a lightly floured surface and knead it gently for about 2 minutes. The dough should then be rolled out, approximately 2 cm thick, and the child can cut out their gingerbread shapes. Place the cut-outs onto the greased baking sheets and decorate by gently pushing raisins into the figures for eyes, mouths and buttons. Then cook on baking trays for 18–20 minutes, or until slightly springy to the touch.

Leave to cool on a wire rack and store for up to 4 days in an airtight container.

Crumble Topping

This was the first recipe I learnt to make as a child. I vividly remember how fun it was to dig my hands into the fat and flour and make a right royal mess.

What you'll need

- 2 oz (50 g) butter
- 4 oz (100 g) plain flour
- 2 oz (50 g) sugar
- Fruit for filling
- Large mixing bowl

What to do

Measure the ingredients with your child and put them into separate bowls. Sit your child on the floor as it is easier for them to get their hands into the mixture this way. Put the butter and flour in a large bowl, which they can have on their laps or just in front of them, and show them how to rub the ingredients together to make a breadcrumb-like mixture – tell them they are making rain! When a dry, crumbly mixture is formed and there are no lumps, have your child stir the sugar in well.

To make the filling prepare whichever fruit you wish to use and place it in the bottom of the baking dish. Apples with a sprinkling of cinnamon go down a treat with children. Simply put a peeled and chopped cooking apple into a saucepan with a little butter, sugar and cinnamon and heat gently until very soft.

Help your child to cover the dish with the crumble topping. Bake at 180 °C for about 20 minutes, or until the topping is golden. Ice cream or custard goes perfectly with it.

Marzipan Fruit

Children love to eat sweet things, but the long lists of additives in mass-produced treats can be detrimental to their health. With these sweet recipes, you know exactly what is going into the goodies.

What you'll need

- A standard-sized block of marzipan
- Food colouring
- Kitchen utensils to create patterns
- Cloves
- Caster sugar to decorate

What to do

Cut the marzipan into three or four pieces and put each chunk into a separate bowl with a drop of food colouring to match a fruit of your child's choice (green for apples, red for strawberries and so on). Mix with a wooden spoon – marzipan is quite stiff so some elbow grease will be needed!

Help your child to mould walnut-sized pieces of coloured marzipan into fruit shapes (e.g. globes for apples or oranges). Create peel for the oranges by gently rolling the marzipan globe over the smallest holes of a grater. For raspberries roll the marzipan piece over a sieve, pressing slightly harder than for the orange. To frost the fruits roll them in caster sugar. Place a clove in the top of the oranges and apples to make the stalks. Add small pieces of green marzipan to create the tops of the strawberries.

Now they are ready to eat, or place them in an airtight box with greaseproof paper to present as a gift for family or friends.

OUT AND ABOUT

Castles

Children love the eerie, grand nature of castles, but as with all outings can quickly become bored if their active minds are not kept occupied. Before the trip, see if you can get your hands on a picture of the castle (or, failing that, any castle) and tell your child to copy it using pencil and paper. Make sure they include typical features, such as a moat, tiny windows and a drawbridge. Once at the castle, help your child to label each part of their drawing as you go round, making a note of what the features are called and what they were used for. This simple activity will bring a centuries-old fortress to life.

Don't forget to find out if the castle has a family friendly area, as these often allow children to touch and feel relics such as chain mail. Only by wearing or even just trying to lift a piece of this medieval battle garment can you understand the great feat it was to fight in full armour.

Mini Marzipan Battenburg

Here's another treat your child can proudly say they made entirely by themselves.

What you'll need

- A block of marzipan
- Food colouring (1–2 drops of each colour)

What to do

Split the block of marzipan in half. Cover one half in cling film to stop it drying out. Split the second half into four equal sized rectangular bars and colour as for 'Marzipan Fruit'. Roll each colour out gently and mould it back into its original bar shape – cut to achieve square edges if necessary. Put the rectangular bars back together in a two-by-two Battenburg style, each bar being next to one of a different colour. Very gently bind them together using a rolling pin.

Take the other piece of marzipan out of its cling film and roll it out thinly to a large rectangle. Wrap this around the chequered block and moisten slightly with cold water to seal.

Slice carefully and thinly for a very sweet treat!

Peanut Butter Creams

These deliciously sweet creams will keep for up to 4 days.

What you'll need

- 4 oz (100 g) soft cheese
- 1 lb 2 oz (550 g) icing sugar, sieved
- 3 oz (75 g) smooth peanut butter
- 1 oz (25 g) butter
- Vanilla essence (1-2 drops)
- 3 oz (75 g) finely chopped peanuts (unsalted)

What to do

Beat the cheese with a wooden spoon until soft and smooth. Gradually beat in the sugar, peanut butter, butter and vanilla essence. It should make a stiff consistency; if not, add more icing sugar until it does. Wrap the mixture in cling film and put it in the fridge for about 2 hours.

Help your child break off small pieces of the resulting fondant and form into ten-pence-sized balls. Roll the balls in the peanuts. These should be stored in cake cases or on greaseproof paper in the fridge. Remove from the fridge an hour before serving.

QUICK IDEA

Secret Messages

To help your child improve their letter sounds and spelling skills, create secret code messages. Instead of writing the message through letters and words in the usual way, replace these with pictures: draw an eye for the letter 'I', a cup for 'drink', and a knot for 'not'. For older children, step things up a notch. For example, for the word 'blink', draw a sink and then beside it write and cross out the letter 'S' and add the letters 'BL'.

Once they have the idea, it's their turn to send you a secret message.

PARTY GAMES

Every now and again I find myself in charge of other children as well as my own, but thankfully I have discovered some group activities which are the perfect way to keep them all amused (and out of trouble). The following are games that my son and his friends ask to play again and again.

Find Your Way Home

This is a fun game to play, and one that started my son on his never-ending quest to create and solve mazes. It requires concentration, but is quickly mastered.

What you'll need

- Two pieces of A3 paper or card
- A pencil
- A ruler
- A felt-tip pen

What to do

With the pencil and ruler, help your child divide one of the pieces of paper into 64 (8 by 8) squares. Ask them to mark the top left square 'Start' and the bottom right square 'Finish'. This is now the board.

Divide the second piece of paper into squares in exactly the same way. Copying the diagram, draw the pattern of semi and full circles, crosses and lines. Cut this sheet of paper into 64 separate squares. These are your counters.

The game can be played with up to three people and the aim is to create a path from the Start square to the Finish square using the lines on the counters. Turn the counters over, blank side up, and choose an equal number each, leaving none remaining. Then players look at their counters but without letting anyone else see. The first player should put down one of their counters at the Start square and then the second player puts one of theirs on a joining square, making sure the black lines on each counter meet. You can only put a counter down that continues a path. If you cannot continue a path, you forfeit that go.

The player to lay a counter on the Finish square wins.

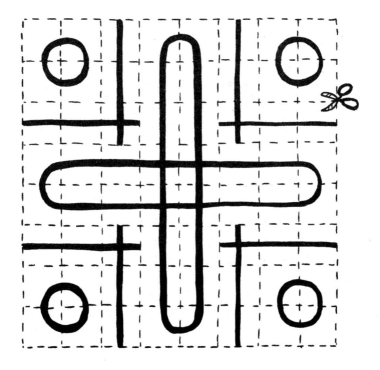

Table Shove Penny

This is a game my son is convinced he invented one stormy spring afternoon.

What you'll need

- A smooth table top (cleared of all objects)
- Lots of pennies
- One larger coin, e.g. a two-pence piece

What to do

To play, get the youngest child to place the larger coin near the edge of the table and then bang the heel of their hand against that edge – gently! – so the coin is 'shoved' along the table. This is the marker coin. The aim of the game is (like bowls) to get your coins closer to the marker coin than your friends.

Each player takes a turn at shoving his or her pennies from the same starting point to as close to the marker coin as possible. The owner of the closest coin wins.

Window Bingo

In this game, the player is aiming to spot everyday items instead of numbers. A great game for younger children, it was once the only way of keeping my son sitting still for five minutes at a time!

What you'll need

- Sheets of paper – A4 is ideal
- Pens

What to do

Draw lines on a piece of paper to divide it into six equal squares. Either you or a child can then draw or write something in each box that might be seen from your window (be sure to choose things which are highly likely to be seen). This is a game board for one player. Create a game board for each child playing – you can use the same pictures on each card, but be sure to mix up the order in which they appear.

Some ideas of things to draw:
- An umbrella
- A red car
- A lorry

- A pair of blue trainers
- A large dog
- A black cat

Sit the children in front of the window and as they see each item they must cross them off their cards. The winner is the first person to get a line of three items crossed off their card.

OUT AND ABOUT

Make a Map

On any outward journey, but preferably one you take fairly regularly, encourage your child to keep their eyes peeled for landmarks such as war memorials, unconventional-looking buildings, or animals in a field. They will need to remember which order they see them in so they can draw them when you reach your destination. Alternatively, you could write down what they see (as long as you aren't driving!).

When you arrive help your child to draw the map and get them to add the landmarks in the appropriate places. If you are returning by the same route, give your child the map and ask them to help direct you back. Otherwise have them create a new map for the way home and be 'navigator' next time you take the trip. With your child's eyes firmly on the road, the usual travel sickness problems may be avoided, and your son or daughter will love telling you what's coming up – and being right!

Adventure Games

My son loves the old adventure game show *The Crystal Maze*, so one rainy afternoon we set about recreating the games, which tested teams in skill, mental and physical categories. Contestants were given timed tests, selected by themselves from the various categories. If completed correctly a crystal was won, and if unsuccessful the contestant found him- or herself locked in. At the end of the games, the number of crystals won determined how much time was spent in the Crystal Dome, where remaining contestants grabbed airborne golden tickets, leading to a prize.

Naturally, it isn't possible to create themed rooms or elaborate tests for your games but with a little imagination you can manage to have several hours of fun. This is also an excellent way of getting siblings to work together – and to recognise each other's skills rather than weaknesses.

What you'll need

- Household items such as pillows, toys, bottles, string or wool
- Paper
- Pens
- A watch with a second hand, or an egg timer

Skill Games

These usually require specific skills such as strength or steady hands – not easy when under pressure. For example:

- Build a vehicle out of selected bits of Lego.
- Fill in the missing pieces of a labyrinth to make a marble run its course (see 'Marble Maze').
- Throw mini beanbags into different sized containers (e.g. empty plant pot, saucepan, laundry basket).
- Fill some jars with water to create a musical scale and then empty one of them – the child must fill it him- or herself to find the missing note.

Mental Games

These are probably the easiest to create as they require fewest props. This doesn't necessarily make them easy to carry out, however. Ideas include:

- Write a word or a phrase onto a sheet of paper or card, cut the letters or words out and shuffle them around – the children merely have to rearrange the pieces of card to recreate the word or phrase.
- Write a message as for the 'Secret Messages'

activity (draw an eye for 'I', a cup of tea for 'T' etc.) to tell them where an item, e.g. a star, is hidden in the room.

- Cut out pictures of items that could be put together to make another word or phrase – e.g. egg and cup, car and boot, shoe and lace, and so on. Put the pictures face up but in a mixed up order and give them one example to show them what they have to do.
- Write out sums on pieces of paper and leave gaps for your child to fill in (perhaps the addition symbol, or one of the numbers).

Physical Games
These are the most popular by far as they can involve lots of jumping and climbing. Ideas include:

- Give a child two cushions and tell them to retrieve e.g. a star from the far end of the room – but if they touch the carpet they forfeit the game.
- Give a child a balloon and make them cross the room using randomly placed cushions as stepping stones, and without letting the balloon touch the floor.
- Create a large enough loop of string or wool to go around a child from head to toe and get

them to use it like a hamster wheel: they must only tread on the wool or string to get from one end of the room to the other.

QUICK IDEA

Mr Wiggly Toes!

This is along the same lines as 'What the Moon Said'. However, instead of writing a story take it in turns to draw a person, leaving a bit of the drawing visible after each turn so the next person can see where to draw from. The sillier the drawing the better – try, for example, clown hats, chain mail, tutus, army boots. Include:

- A hat
- The head
- The body
- The legs
- The feet

Get the group to pick a name for the colourful character, such as Mr Wiggly Toes, before finally unravelling their work of art.

Pin the Nose on Daddy

This is a variation on the traditional 'pin the tail on the donkey' game. In our house Daddy usually ends up with huge moustaches and ridiculous glasses. You could use a picture of your child, a famous pop star or a children's TV character instead.

What you'll need

- 2 large (e.g. A4) photos or pictures – one of Daddy and one of somebody else
- A notice board
- Drawing pins
- A blindfold (e.g. a tea towel)

Pin the photo of Daddy to the board. Cut out the nose/lips/headwear/facial hair from the second photo. Alternatively you can draw facial hair or a silly hat and cut that out. Pierce the cut-out with the drawing pin. Blindfold the child and turn them round two or three times to disorientate them. Give them the cut-out very carefully, making sure they have got hold of the pinhead so they won't prick their fingers. Now they must try to pin the facial feature in the appropriate place on the photo of Daddy. The person with the best placed feature wins.

Fish Race

This is a traditional parlour game, but can be made more fun by creating shapes other than fish – for instance, a favourite animal or vehicle.

What you'll need

- Lots of newspaper
- Scissors

What to do

Cut out a fish shape (about A4 size) from a single sheet of newspaper for every player. Get each player to decorate or name their fish, and lay them in a line at one end of the room. Designate a finishing line – perhaps just the wall on the other side. Give each player a folded newspaper. On starter's orders, players must frantically wave their newspapers up and down behind their fish to create a breeze and send their contestant swimming along the floor. The first fish to reach the finishing line wins.

The Tidy-Up Game

As parents we lead very busy lives and it's important for children to realise it's their responsibility to clear up after themselves. I devised this game not only as a housework aid but also to help my son learn his colours and letter sounds.

What you'll need

- A messy room!

What to do

Your child's bedroom or play area is a great place to start as the mess will be made up of your child's belongings and so they are more likely to be familiar with their names. Tell your child that they are only to put away toys of a certain colour or which start with a certain letter. For example all the green toys or all those which start with a 'b' ('bear', 'bunny', 'ball'). Help them initially; they will very quickly pick up on the idea of the game.

For some healthy competition, get your child to choose a letter for himself or herself and also for you or another child, and then race to see who can put the most away, counting each toy as it finds its way into its box or cupboard. The person who puts the most items away is the winner.

QUICK IDEA

Create a Crossword

If you are feeling creative yourself, devise a crossword in readiness for a long journey, particularly on a plane or a train. Alternatively this can be another activity that you can do with your child, as a present for a friend or relative.

When thinking of words, remember the more personal they are to your child the better. Use names of friends or toys, or words associated with a hobby or holiday you have taken. To begin with, write your first word and then (as in Scrabble) add other words to it going up, down or across. Do the same to each of those words until you feel your crossword is big enough. Keep hold of this to give your child as an answer sheet, but now on a new sheet of paper, recreate the crossword using empty boxes instead of the letters. Then create your clues and write these underneath – the older your child the more cryptic the clue can be. Anagrams are also suitable for older children.

Hot Potato

This is another very simple game that can be made as challenging as you feel the children can enjoy.

What you'll need

- Two people
- A ball (a tennis ball is ideal)

What to do

Sit facing your child with your legs slightly apart and your feet touching (making a diamond shape). Roll the ball to each other and as you roll the ball away, say 'Hot potato' as if the ball is in fact a very hot potato and burning your fingers.

After a few rolls, instead of saying 'Hot potato' you can say words that rhyme, such as cat, bat, hat and so on. You can also play the alphabet game. Pick a category such as girls' names and with each roll of the ball you must say a girl's name from the next letter of the alphabet: Annabelle, Becky, Charlotte and so on. Another variation for older children is to choose an end or beginning sound such as 'end' (as in bend, mend, send) or 'th' (as in the, them, those).

Put on a Show

Children are, on the whole, natural exhibitionists and enjoy the attention and applause of their families. Creating, costuming and choreographing a show is a fun way to spend a day, and the results of everyone's efforts are always enchanting and often utterly hilarious.

What you'll need

- A CD player
- Dressing up outfits and accessories
- Household items

What to do

Discuss what is to be performed; perhaps a story or even a comic sketch or a song and dance routine. With smaller children keeping it as simple as possible is the key to its success. Then work out how you are going to tell the story through actions, with, optionally, you or one of the children narrating. Help them use their surroundings to their advantage, such as a door between two rooms to create separate stage and off-stage areas, and using furniture as props. Consider what music from your CD collection could be used to dramatic effect, and assist with the costumes – even a simple hat or coat can effectively create a whole new character.

Encourage as much rehearsing as possible. A shy child could help with prompting or directing. Then invite the 'audience' to take a seat and be entertained, ensuring everyone laughs in all the right places and applauds loudly at every opportunity.

TOP TIP

The children could create programmes for their audience, with a colourful drawing on the front and a cast list on the reverse. On the inside, a synopsis of the story should be written, even broken down into three 'Acts' if appropriate.

OUT AND ABOUT

Make a Map

On any outward journey, but preferably one you take fairly regularly, encourage your child to keep their eyes peeled for landmarks such as war memorials, unconventional-looking buildings, or animals in a field. They will need to remember which order they see them in so they can draw them when you reach your destination. Alternatively, you could write down what they see (as long as you aren't driving!).

When you arrive help your child to draw the map and get them to add the landmarks in the appropriate places. If you are returning by the same route, give your child the map and ask them to help direct you back. Otherwise have them create a new map for the way home and be 'navigator' next time you take the trip. With your child's eyes firmly on the road, the usual travel sickness problems may be avoided, and your son or daughter will love telling you what's coming up – and being right!

GARDEN FUN

No matter how bad the weather, my son loves the outdoors. In a bid to keep him happy – and dry – I encourage a compromise on damp days and we begin one of the following ideas. Gardening in the warm and dry has to be one of my favourite ways to spend a wintry afternoon.

Rosalie's Bird Feeder

I have a lovely friend called Rosalie who is never happier than when outdoors with her children. She came up with this idea one cold winter's afternoon when it was too ghastly even for her to venture outside.

What you'll need

- A blunt-ended needle (darning or embroidery)
- A length of string
- A bag of monkey nuts
- A clothes peg

What to do

Show your child how to make a hole carefully in the centre of the shell (in between the two nuts) and get your child to thread the string through until there is a long line of peanuts. Tie a knot in one end of the string. Attach the other end of the string to a peg and fix it somewhere high in the garden like a washing line. Wait for the birds to come!

Feeding Ball

This is a very simple idea that's a perfect, ecological way to get rid of leftover food.

What you'll need

- A medium block of lard
- A length of string
- Some scraps of food (e.g. peelings, crusts) whizzed in a food processor
- Some wild bird seed

What to do

Heat the lard on a medium heat until it is soft and gooey, and then get your child to tip and mix in the food scraps and bird seed. Stir them in – all the scraps will need to be blended with the lard. After the mixture has cooled slightly (check it's cool enough to touch) ask your child to use their hands to shape the goo around the string into a ball shape (like soap on a rope). Sit the feeding ball on a plate until it hardens and then attach it somewhere like a washing line or a branch for the birds. Make sure your child washes their hands in plenty of handwash!

Rain Catcher

My son watched the weather forecast one day and was shocked to hear that two inches of rain had fallen overnight. Fascinated by the fact that such data could be collected, we worked on building our very own – yet somewhat less hi-tech – equipment.

What you'll need

- A plastic beaker or cup with straight sides
- Food colouring
- A ruler
- A pen

What to do

Using a ruler and a pen, clearly mark the side of the beaker at half-centimetre intervals. Put a tiny drop of food colouring into the bottom of the beaker so that the measurements are easier to read. Put the measuring cup outside, somewhere open and away from overhanging rooves and gutters; for example, on a chair or table on the patio.

You can check how fast the rain is falling as frequently as you like – on a particularly wet day it can rain several centimetres in an hour – just remember to empty the cup after each check. Older children might like to make a graph or keep a diary of the rainfall to see how bad the weather has really been.

QUICK IDEA

Post-It Note Alphabet Game

A great game for encouraging younger children to learn their letter sounds. Choose a letter sound of which plenty of examples can be found around your house, for example T ('table', 'television', 'telephone'). Give your child a pack of Post-It notes or similar and a pen and tell them to go from room to room finding things that begin with that letter sound. Each item found should be labelled by your child with the sticky note and the letter marked clearly on it.

Make a Grass Ball

This was one of those 'I wonder if that would work' ideas that seem to pop into my mind when I am supposed to be concentrating on something else! Your child's little hands are perfect for getting the soil into the ball.

What you'll need

- A plastic washing powder ball
- A packet of grass seeds
- Empty ice cream tub
- Soil
- A skewer
- Small watering can

What to do

Make lots of holes in the ball using the skewer. Ask your child to mix the seeds with the soil in an ice cream tub (using their hands) and then fill the plastic ball with the mixture. Give it a really good water over the sink and keep it on a window ledge or in a conservatory, turning it occasionally so that each side is given light and the chance to grow. Water it regularly and within a few weeks you will have a thriving grass ball.

Sunflower Race

When we moved house, my friend Rosalie presented my son and me with our very own sunflower race kit as a house-warming gift. This is a great ongoing activity for the long summer holidays – which, in this country, always include the odd rainy day.

What you'll need

- Sunflower seeds (from a garden centre)
- Soil
- Seedling pots
- Small address labels

What to do

Get each child to choose a seed and plant it in the seedling pot with some soil. Put a label on the pot so that they know which is theirs. Water them regularly and keep them in a sunny place, and very quickly they will start to grow. Once big enough they can be replanted outside and at the end of the summer the person with the tallest sunflower wins.

OUT AND ABOUT

Park Fun

Have your child draw a picture of an imaginary park keeper with slightly larger than usual accessories, such as keys, bucket and watch, and give their creation a name. Come up with a few questions and write them on the relevant part of the park keeper drawing.

For example:

- On his watch: Mr Blimp says the park opens at midnight and closes at 4 a.m. Is he right?
- On the bucket: Mr Blimp needs to clean the war memorial, but doesn't know where it is – can you find it for him?
- On his keys: Mr Blimp says that there are 8 entrances to the park. Is that true?

If it really is too wet to go out, preparing the activity will keep your child busy and they can even come up with some of the questions themselves, as it doesn't really matter if you know the answers or not before going to the park.

Internet Resources

While we cannot guarantee the safety of any of the activities or content on these websites, with some parental common sense you should be able to find plenty of help below if you become really stuck on a rainy day.

Printouts for art work and arty ideas:
www.preschoolprintables.com
www.activityvilliage.co.uk
www.dltk-kids.com/crafts/

Learning fun:
www.chaosscience.org.uk
www.rsc.org
www.woodlands-junior.kent.sch.uk

For games:
www.playmobil.co.uk
www.hotwheels.com
www.bbc.co.uk/cbeebies
www.thunderbirdsonline.com
www.hasbro.com/monkeybar/
www.uk.barbie.com
www.pollypocket.com

Other books from Summersdale

THE
CHEMICAL
MAZE

SHOPPING COMPANION

Your guide to food additives and cosmetic ingredients

BILL STATHAM

The Chemical Maze Shopping Companion
Your Guide to Food Additives and Cosmetic Ingredients

Bill Statham

£5.99

Tartrazine, polydextrose and E133 – how are you supposed to know what's dangerous and what's not? The warnings we receive daily about chemicals used in our food and cosmetics can be overwhelming and confusing.

This user-friendly pocket shopping guide tells you at a glance which additives are hazardous, which chemicals are best avoided and which ingredients are safe, making it easier to shop for your family.

The colour-coded, alphabetical tables provide valuable information about potential health effects and take the mystery out of additive codes, helping you to choose which product to put in your basket and which to leave on the shelf.

☺☺ This book may seriously improve your health.

Bill Statham is a researcher and writer in health education who studied and practised homeopathy in the UK and Australia for over ten years. He has found that eliminating certain chemicals from your life can significantly benefit your health.

Baby tips
for mums

Simon Brett
Bestselling author of *How to be a Little Sod*

Baby tips
for dads

Simon Brett
Bestselling author of *How to be a Little Sod*

Baby tips
for grandparents

Simon Brett
Bestselling author of *How to be a Little Sod*

Simon Brett

£4.99 each

Whether you are a new mum, rookie dad or seasoned grandparent of a lively horde, make these little books the latest additions to your household.

www.summersdale.com